N

Mark A. Villano, CSP

LITURGICAL PRESS
Collegeville, Minnesota
litpress.org

Nihil Obstat: Rev. Robert C. Harren, J.C.L., *Censor Librorum*
Imprimatur: ✠ Most Rev. Patrick M. Neary, C.S.C., Bishop of St. Cloud, July 3, 2025

Cover design by Monica Bokinskie.
Cover art courtesy of Getty Images.

ISSN: 1552-8782; 2692-6407 (e-book)
ISBN: 979-8-4008-0155-6 979-8-4008-0157-0 (ebook)

Introduction

As a kid, I never looked forward to Lent. It was the time when we were supposed to give up stuff we liked. Who looks forward to that? At some point, though, I learned the meaning of the word "Lent." It comes from an old English word meaning "springtime." It refers to the lengthening of days, the increase of sunshine.

Trudging through the winter months in Connecticut, I finally had a reason to look forward to Lent! This is a season of renewal, of growth. Just as the earth seems to "wake up" during spring, we're called to wake up to the Spirit.

There's another word I never liked as a kid: discipline. Discipline was an external concept to me. It was something that was done *to* me. Then, at some point, I discovered another kind of discipline. This kind was not external but came from within. It was *self*-discipline. It was a tool for growth.

Even as kids we could understand that good outcomes often required tradeoffs. Practicing a musical instrument or training for a sport involved discipline, but we knew it would pay off in the future. As adults we deepen that awareness. We set life goals and follow through on them even when it seems difficult. We learn the meaning of love, not only as something spontaneous and "fun," but as something that requires discipline for the sake of another's good.

Self-discipline is part of Lent. But so are celebration and joy. St. Teresa of Avila, the great Spanish mystic, is credited with saying: "There's a time for penance, and a time for partridge." In other words, there's a time for fasting and a time for feasting. One does not fast for its own sake. One fasts for the greater good that comes from it. We fast for the sake of the feast. And during Lent, there is time for both penance and partridge.

Lent is springtime for the soul. Whatever the Spirit is leading you to do or give up or add to your life this Lent, follow that call. And when Easter comes, we'll be ready to celebrate because we'll be awake. We'll be renewed, our hearts alive, ready for the feast.

Fr. Mark Villano, CSP

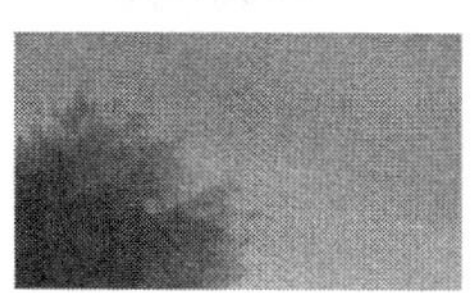

REFLECTIONS

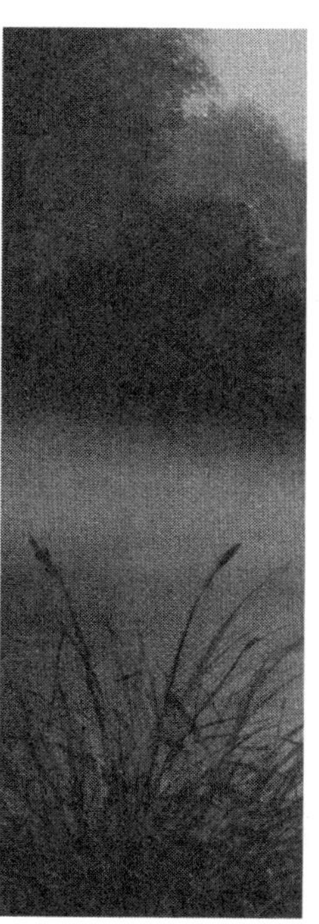

This Is the Time

Readings: Joel 2:12-18; 2 Cor 5:20–6:2; Matt 6:1-6, 16-18

Scripture:
We are ambassadors for Christ, as if God were appealing through us. We implore you on behalf of Christ, be reconciled to God. (2 Cor 5:20)

Reflection: There are times when, physically, we know something just isn't right, but we can't put our finger on it. We don't feel right. We're tired. We start to think of the ways we haven't been taking care of ourselves. Sometimes we ignore the little warnings our body tries to give us. At other times we think, *I need to get back on track.*

This doesn't only happen in our physical lives. It happens in our emotional, relational, and spiritual lives, too. They're all connected, aren't they? If one part of us gets thrown off, the other parts can feel it, too. We are whole persons: body, mind, and spirit. And sometimes it's our spirit that gives the warning. Our spirit, speaking from the true depth of our lives, calls us to pay attention, to remember who we are, and to consider what is most important in life. It impels us to search out the meaning in St. Paul's words: "[B]e reconciled to God."

Jesus' words from the Sermon on the Mount, proclaimed in our churches on Ash Wednesday, warn us about what deadens the spirit or soul. There are signs of this "deadening": doing things just for others to see, doing things to gain applause or human approval, seeking only superficial rewards. We begin to live in a falseness, an illusion. We may not notice it at first, but our soul is crying out. It's starving. It wants to get back on track.

Is your soul crying out? Are you looking for a fuller, deeper life? Then this is the acceptable time (2 Cor 6:2)! Don't let it pass you by. Start feeding your soul. Embark on this journey called Lent.

Meditation: Preparation is important when beginning any journey. We plan, we gather provisions. What do I want to carry with me during the days ahead? What prayer exercises or spiritual practices will accompany me?

Prayer: Lord, I want more than a superficial life, more than paying lip service to my beliefs and values. Help me to answer the call of Lent to prayer, fasting, and service. I want to savor the depth within me and live from that depth.

Choose

Readings: Deut 30:15-20; Luke 9:22-25

Scripture:
"If anyone wishes to come after me, he must deny himself and take up his cross daily and follow me." (Luke 9:23)

Reflection: When we hear Jesus calling us to "deny" ourselves, do we hear it as a self-effacement, a denial of our worth? It may sound like we're being asked to put ourselves down in some way. Is that what God wants?

Of course not! You are a child of God, beloved of the Father. Your life is a gift willed by God for the good of all. There is a human tendency, though, to turn in on ourselves. Everything becomes about us. The world revolves around us: what we want, what others can do for us. When life is all about building up our own ego, we become smaller, impoverished. The result is a distortion of ourselves and our world.

That is what needs to be put to death. That's the "self" we need to lose in order to find our *true* self. When we accept the gift of our lives in relationship to the One who loved us into being, we begin to see things as they really are. We set out on a new path with the Lord as our guide and companion. We give ourselves to others in love and service. The world opens up to us in a new way. It becomes larger, enriched.

Today we're offered the same choice that has echoed through the ages. We hear it in the ancient plea of God to his chosen ones: "I have set before you life and death, the blessing and the curse" (Deut 30:19). Choose your identity as a beloved child of God. Choose to live in that enlarged, enriched world. Choose life!

Meditation: What does it mean to "choose life" in the small, ordinary decisions and tasks that fill my days? When a friend has hurt me, when someone I know needs help, or when I'm trying to decide what to do for Lent, can I see the connection between small choices and the big choice to follow Christ?

Prayer: Lord, my choice to follow you is being played out in the moments of my everyday reality. Help me discover and follow your path this day, and so find my true self in you.

Fast and Feast

Readings: Isa 58:1-9a; Matt 9:14-15

Scripture:
"Can the wedding guests mourn as long as the bridegroom is with them?" (Matt 9:15)

Reflection: John the Baptist's disciples are a little confused about Jesus' disciples and their religious practices. Why don't Jesus' disciples fast like they do? Jesus has a great comeback to this question: *No one fasts during a wedding banquet.*

Jesus obviously saw great value in fasting. He spent forty days in the desert praying and fasting in preparation for his public ministry. Yet he often encountered people who were preoccupied with external religious observances but had lost touch with the meaning of those practices. People often keep traditions for traditions' sake, rather than for the sake of their meaning and value.

The prophet Isaiah dealt with the same problem in his day: "[Y]our fast ends in quarreling and fighting" (Isa 58:4). He called out these sinful practices and went on to say that the kind of fast that pleases God involves setting the oppressed free and reaching out to those in need. There's a communal nature to our fasting. To care about our own spiritual health while ignoring the world around us would not make much sense to Isaiah.

Perhaps we can consider how fasting may free us for some kind of service. Money saved by fasting can be applied to a charity fund, or time saved by forgoing an activity we like can be offered to someone who could use our help.

Our Lenten fasting—whether it be from food, small luxuries, or destructive habits—must be joined to a sincere heart to be pleasing to God. True fasting opens us to our radical dependence on God and to greater sensitivity to the needs of others. That's how it becomes an act of worship. That's how it changes our hearts and prepares us for the feast of Easter.

Meditation: Do I see the "feast" in the "fast"? How can I offer to the Lord the kind of fasting Jesus performed, directed wholly to God rather than myself? Am I aware of the needs of my neighbors and open to the sacrifice of my time, presence, or resources to assist them?

Prayer: Lord, you are the bridegroom who invites us to the heavenly banquet. Purify my heart during this penitential season, so I can more fully embrace your call and share in your love.

Lightning

Readings: Isa 58:9b-14; Luke 5:27-32

Scripture:
He said to him, "Follow me." And leaving everything behind, he got up and followed him. (Luke 5:27-28)

Reflection: Anyone who loves words or engages in creative writing can appreciate this quote attributed to Mark Twain: "The difference between the almost right word and the right word is the difference between the lightning bug and the lightning." Maybe you've had that experience when struggling to express yourself. You know a word you're using just doesn't capture the nuance you're trying to convey. Even a thesaurus doesn't satisfy. You step away from the page, hoping some distance and subconscious brooding will help. You come back, and then it happens: The perfect word flashes in your mind. Lightning strikes!

There are much bigger experiences in life where metaphorical lightning bursts into our consciousness. These are conversion experiences. The Greek word *metanoia*, meaning "to change one's mind," expresses their power. We transcend or move beyond the way we are accustomed to thinking to a greater awareness. Conversion can touch all areas of our life: personal, relational, moral, spiritual. Sometimes reaching a certain developmental stage readies us to receive life-changing insights. Sometimes unexpected life events (moving to a new place, falling in love, the birth of a baby, the death of a loved one) prepare us for ongoing conversion.

In today's Gospel, Levi is sitting at his post, doing the same work he has always done, thinking with the same mind that has settled him in his role, his fixed way of relating to himself and others. Then the eyes of Jesus meet his. A presence is sensed: the One who knows him as he is and loves him as he is. A voice breaks through: *Follow me.*

Grace has prepared him for this. He responds. Life changes. Lightning has struck.

Meditation: What times of conversion in my life have brought new insights or set me on a new path? Were these times of personal struggle? Joyful events? Hearing the word of God? Experiences of community? Moments of deep prayer? Did these moments come suddenly, or did they develop slowly over time?

Prayer: Lord, thank you for the times when your voice was clear and renewed my mind and heart. Continue to give me strength and hope as I follow your path.

Worship

Readings: Gen 2:7-9; 3:1-7; Rom 5:12-19 or 5:12, 17-19; Matt 4:1-11

Scripture:
"The Lord, your God, shall you worship / and him alone shall you serve." (Matt 4:10; Deut 6:13)

Reflection: The origin of the word "worship" is rooted in the concept of worthiness. Where do I place worth? What is worthy of my life? What do I reverence with my time, my attention, my skill? Where I find worth will determine where I go in life—where I spend my time, devote my energy, and develop my gifts.

Our first parents in the Garden of Eden were assured of God's love for them, but they were tempted to think that wasn't enough. We, too, are sometimes tempted to think that God's love is not enough to sustain our lives.

When love is not enough, we look to other things to worship. We may look to the acquisition of money and material things to sustain our lives. But then we need more money and more things to gratify us. Acquisition becomes a compulsion. We are no longer stewards in the garden, but addicts.

When love is not enough, we may turn to achievement or power to satisfy us. Achievements are then no longer about mastering ourselves or finding worthy goals. Achievement, position, and power become all about control. We drag others down to elevate ourselves. We seek titles to feel superior.

When love is not enough, we may seek the attention of others to validate ourselves. Instead of seeking to be known, understood, or accepted, we seek attention to gain others' approval. Attention, reputation, and honor become exercises in fleeting self-importance.

Acquisition, achievement, control, approval, honor—none of these things have the power to save us. On the cross Jesus was stripped of all of it. He even felt abandoned. And yet he worshipped. He found his worth in the love of God. He began a new story in a new garden, the garden of the empty tomb, and became the source of salvation for us all.

Meditation: How do I express what is of most worth to me? Have I found worthy life goals? How am I serving God's love, sharing my gifts, and helping my neighbor?

Prayer: Lord, open my mind and heart to see that you are worthy to receive all glory, reverence, and worship. May this awareness free me to live more fully in your presence.

Works of Mercy

Readings: Lev 19:1-2, 11-18; Matt 25:31-46

Scripture:
" 'When did we see you a stranger and welcome you, or naked and clothe you?' " (Matt 25:38)

Reflection: My parish recently decided to structure its teen Confirmation program in a unique way by organizing it around the traditional corporal and spiritual works of mercy. In the first year of preparation, students discuss topics related to the corporal works, and in the second year, the spiritual works.

Now, you'd think today's Gospel reading, which names the corporal works of mercy, would fit in only with the first year's schedule. These are active, physical, immediate kinds of undertakings, like visiting the sick. As someone once said: "To the hungry, God comes as bread." Yet, each of the corporal works includes a spiritual work as well.

I was asked to speak to the teens about "clothing the naked" as an act of mercy. First, I spoke about the physical needs of each of us. I asked them to think about how their parents literally dressed them as children and still provide for them. I pointed to the clothing drives we hold at the parish that supply the St. Vincent DePaul Society's thrift store in our city. That store not only helps people who have limited clothing budgets, but it also supports the Society's other charitable works.

But then I asked the teens to consider other ways people feel naked, exposed, or vulnerable. Students who are coming into a new school may not feel accepted. Others may feel humiliated by social media bullying. They need to be "clothed with dignity." Or, when we ourselves feel weak or powerless to change things for the better, we need to remind ourselves that we are "clothed with power" by the Holy Spirit that Christ sends to us.

The corporal and the spiritual go together. We are body and soul. And so is our neighbor.

Meditation: Sometimes people hunger for bread; sometimes they hunger for meaning. Sometimes people literally thirst for water; at other times they thirst for the milk of human kindness. How can I reach out in mercy to those God has put on my path?

Prayer: O Lord, free me to both give and receive works of mercy. May I always be aware of the mercy you lavish on your children, and may I do what I can to imitate you.

Praying with the Word

Readings: Isa 55:10-11; Matt 6:7-15

Scripture:
"In praying, do not babble . . ." (Matt 6:7)

Reflection: Estimates of how many advertisements people are exposed to daily vary greatly, but there is no doubt that "message clutter" is real. There are so many avenues through which to receive ads these days: television, radio, print and digital news, entertainment channels, billboards, bumper stickers, T-shirts, mugs, etc. We manage to tune out most of it. (How loud or glitzy must an ad be to stand out?) Still, that's a lot of "babble."

Sometimes we need to turn off the noise. We need time in our day when we simply allow ourselves to "be" and to listen to the silence where God's voice is heard. Our stance in such times is: "Lord, you are here. I am yours. Be with me." In that place, there is no need to babble on. We don't have to be glamorous or glitzy enough to be heard. God is there for us.

There are also times when we need to turn to words, and there are no better ones than those that flow from the heart. Isaiah reminds us that God's word comes like the rain that softens the earth and makes it fruitful. It achieves the end for which it was sent: to teach us and to save us. Our words can also have powerful effects as they express what is really in our hearts.

Jesus is the Word made flesh. He teaches us today about prayer and invites us into words that flow from his own heart. In the Lord's Prayer, we're not merely imitating Jesus or following instructions. Jesus, the Word, is inviting us into his own prayer, his own intimacy with God. May we never take for granted the privilege, the power, and the communion we have when we pray as the Word taught us.

Meditation: How special it is at Mass when, right before communion, we are called to pray together in the words of our Savior. Are there other times when I feel the desire or need to pray the Lord's Prayer? How does it calm me or challenge me? How does it send me back into my life with a renewed sense of God's loving presence with me?

Prayer: Lord, you are here. I am yours. Be with me.

Signs

Readings: Jonah 3:1-10; Luke 11:29-32

Scripture:
"This generation . . . seeks a sign, but no sign will be given it, except the sign of Jonah." (Luke 11:29)

Reflection: The crowd in today's Gospel seems to be asking for a sign in order to test Jesus. But I can imagine plenty of circumstances where someone might ask God for a sign for more understandable reasons. Someone may be feeling frustrated or at the end of their rope and wants assurance that they will make it through this tough time. Someone else may be humbly realizing that they can't do it all alone anymore, and desperately wants divine help to go on. Another person may know exactly what course of action they want to take and is looking for God's affirmation.

Maybe asking for a sign is just human nature. But no matter the circumstances, Jesus' answer to the untrusting crowd suffices. He basically says to them: *You have your sign already.* And then he reminds them of the story of Jonah.

People in the bustling city of Nineveh were going about their everyday lives. Apparently, they were also in need of deep change. Perhaps coarseness, greed, hatred, or injustice ruled their lives and relationships. Perhaps they were oblivious to the ways their culture had hardened them. Then a prophet, Jonah, came to them saying, "Change your ways!" This foreigner easily could have been ignored or dismissed. But somehow, someway, the people actually heard him. They listened. They recognized God's word being spoken to them, and they acted on it.

We too go about our everyday, ordinary lives without much thought. Sometimes we may be frustrated, sometimes humbled. Perhaps much of the time we are oblivious. But what if, in the midst of all of this, God is sending us signs? What if we are *surrounded* by signs: prophets sharing spiritual insights, stories of repentance and healing, lives changed by the love of Christ? What if this time we actually hear and see and say yes to God's word and follow it? Would we change our ways and become more alive? Would we become signs to those around us?

Meditation: Has my heart hardened in any area of my life? Where do I need change and growth? What signs of God's presence surround me?

Prayer: All-merciful God, help me repent of my sins. Make me a sign of new life and growth.

Seek and Find

Readings: Esth C:12, 14-16, 23-25; Matt 7:7-12

Scripture:
"Help me, who am alone and have no help but you, for I am taking my life in my hand." (Esth C:14-15)

Reflection: In the book of Esther, a young Jewish woman becomes queen in a foreign land. She soon discovers that a member of the king's cabinet wants to destroy her people. So Esther must go to work. She makes a plan, moves into danger, goes into battle. She must use the tools she has to thwart the enemy. In these circumstances, her prayer is truly anguished: *God, I feel so alone; I have no help but you. Help me! I'm taking my life in my hands!*

I remember a time in college when I opened my Bible, and my eyes fell right on this prayer of Esther. I don't remember exactly what I was going through at the time, but I know it was difficult. I felt helpless and lost. I was asking, seeking, knocking, as Jesus bids us to do in the Gospel reading today. Esther's prayer became mine.

Usually we are looking for calm, serene experiences of prayer. And there's beauty in that. But prayers like Esther's—prayers of anguish and desperation, cries from the heart when things look bleak—these prayers are beautiful as well. We can all relate to those feelings at various times in our lives.

Even when we are going through bleak or questioning times, we are called to keep the lines of communication open with God. Ask, seek, knock. Cry out! The relationship with God that these prayers express is what helps us pass through such times. These prayers help us expand our hearts. They compel us to grow. They ultimately lead to deeper trust in a loving Father who, as Jesus assures us, wants to give us bread, not stones.

Meditation: When have circumstances caused me to storm heaven with my prayers? How did God's answer come to me? What shape did it take? Was another person part of God's answer? When have I been the answer to someone else's prayer?

Prayer: Lord, when I feel overwhelmed, let me always remember your abiding presence and your promise of assistance. Help me to seek and find you in all things.

Peace and Justice

Readings: Ezek 18:21-28; Matt 5:20-26

Scripture:
"[L]eave your gift there at the altar, go first and be reconciled with your brother, and then come and offer your gift." (Matt 5:24)

Reflection: One of Pope St. Paul VI's best-known quotes is: "If you want peace, work for justice." I can imagine someone hearing these words for the first time and wondering if they're really true. Do peace and justice really go together this way?

If we think of peace as merely the absence of war, then it may not seem to be so tightly bound to justice. But is that true peace? Couldn't "peace" just be a cover for all kinds of ongoing hatred, resentments, and oppression that simmer beneath the surface? Isn't a tenuous peace just a ceasefire in an ongoing battle? True and lasting peace comes from developing mutual respect among people, a sense of right relationships and order. Without just relationships, violence isn't far behind.

This is not only true among nations. Justice and peace begin in our hearts. In the Sermon on the Mount, Jesus gives his disciples a true orientation, an inner compass, when he teaches that our righteousness is not based on a mere external of the law. True righteousness comes from receiv- ...fe in God's Spirit and turning our thoughts and ... doing God's will. That brings us to the heart of the ... the love of God and neighbor.

W... may not be murdering one another, but that's not enough. Ceasefires aren't enough. Are we truly at peace? Are we reconciled? Even worship can be postponed for the work of reconciliation and peace. As Jesus said, "[L]eave your gift there at the altar, go first and be reconciled."

Peacemaking is a sacred act, inspired in us by the One we worship.

Meditation: Lent is a time to learn more clearly what it means to receive new life. Am I living in the freedom and peace of a child of God? Where do I need to let go of resentments and move on in peace?

Prayer: O God, you ask me to forgive as you forgive. Give me the grace to live as you ask. Help me to be a peacemaker.

Be Perfect

Readings: Deut 26:16-19; Matt 5:43-48

Scripture:
"So be perfect, just as your heavenly Father is perfect." (Matt 5:48)

Reflection: I once preached on these words of Jesus from the Sermon on the Mount and asked the congregation: "So, is anybody here perfect yet?" Thankfully, no one said "Yes." That would've ruined the homily!

Imagine the anxiety it would produce if we thought the Lord expected perfection from us here and now (especially for those of us with a perfectionist streak already!). We know we're not perfect. And Jesus knows that, too. Jesus knows we are always in need. Sometimes I picture Jesus smiling at his disciples as he says these words to them—not because he's not serious, but because he knew them. He knew he could challenge his friends *because* they were his friends.

Think of a coach who urges his or her athletes on: "Because I know you, I know that you can do better. You can be more than you are. Don't sit back and get comfortable. I believe in you!" Or imagine a trusted friend who says, "Hey, what's been happening with you? You've got to get out of this rut. How can I help you get back on track?"

Get motivated. Find a vision. Set goals and move toward them. Act! Perfection may be for heaven, but here and now we are *being perfected*. Our goal as Christians, as disciples of Jesus, is holiness (or another word: wholeness)—to be more merciful, strong, free, faithful, and loving. How do we start? By first receiving God's mercy and love, by reverencing God's holiness.

The good news is that we have a God who calls us friends and is ready to help us. We have a God who believes in us.

Meditation: How am I moving toward my goals this Lent? Are there old habits I want to break or new patterns I want to establish? What step can I take today to move in that direction of wholeness and holiness?

Prayer: Almighty God, I reverence your holiness that made me and redeemed me. I thank you for your friendship that heals and sustains me. May I always feel your companionship, listen for your coaching, and delight in your smile.

The Extraordinary in the Ordinary

Readings: Gen 12:1-4a; 2 Tim 1:8b-10; Matt 17:1-9

Scripture:
And he was transfigured before them; his face shone like the sun . . . (Matt 17:2)

Reflection: I always liked this saying from the East: "After ecstasy, the laundry." There are ordinary experiences, and there are extraordinary experiences. The transfiguration of Jesus certainly falls in the latter category. A special memory is being shared with us—an experience that goes beyond words. When we don't have words, we turn to symbols, images, and poetry.

In this case, the Gospel's description conveys how Jesus is fulfilling the divine promises given to the chosen people through the law and the prophets. The cloud, the voice, the light—these were manifestations of the divine presence when the people came out of Egypt during the exodus. Now, on the Mount of Transfiguration, they are manifestations of how God continues to care for, enlighten, and guide his people through Jesus. The disciples are glimpsing something of God's glory.

Jesus tells the disciples not to talk about the experience yet. People are not ready to hear it. The only way this experience will make sense is in the long run, by coming down the mountain into the ordinary events of life. This is how we begin to see the extraordinary *in* the ordinary. Of course, in the disciples' case, those dusty roads through the valleys will eventually lead to the cross.

That's more than a message for laundry day. Jesus is inviting the disciples (and us) to bring their faith—to bring *him*—not merely into everyday routines but into experiences of rejection, suffering, pain, and abandonment. That's where we'll understand the depth of the healing and love Christ wants to give us.

Thank God for the mountaintop experiences: the retreats, prayer meetings, accomplishments, friendships, and romance. God gives us these gifts to help us glimpse his glory. But it's the harsher realities that test us, purify us, and deepen our understanding. That's where we come to know how close God is. We come to understand the gift in the ordinary.

Meditation: When have I been especially aware of the presence of God? How did I feel? How did it affect my understanding of myself? My daily life? My relationships with others?

Prayer: Lord, be with me as I travel the ordinary path of my life. Let me know in strong and beautiful ways that you travel with me.

Giving and Receiving

Readings: Dan 9:4b-10; Luke 6:36-38

Scripture:
"For the measure with which you measure will in return be measured out to you." (Luke 6:38)

Reflection: It's natural to feel disappointment when our efforts are not recognized, our invitations are not answered, or our need for help is not addressed. We may even wallow at times because of the seeming lack of appreciation for our work or lack of attention to our hardships. But we might ask ourselves: Do we give to others what we want for ourselves?

It sounds so simple. Why is it so difficult to practice at times? Often our eyes are on ourselves and what we lack rather than on others and what we can give. But Jesus reminds us that what we measure out to others returns to us. We've all heard the phrase "What goes around comes around." It's a principle that's recognized by many spiritual traditions. (You've heard of karma, right?) It's not magic. It doesn't show itself instantaneously. But it's true to our experience and teaches us how much we have to give.

Sharing what we wish to receive is a discipline that takes time to develop. It takes spiritual maturity. It's about becoming a certain type of person—the person we want to be—free, open, engaged, compassionate.

Ultimately, we can't give what we haven't received. Lent is a time to remember again what God has given to us, to experience again the love and compassion that is always there for us. We turn to God's word and sacrament, to prayer and listening. We search our hearts and find the love our Creator has placed there. This is the beginning of giving.

We're empowered by love to give love. And we'll notice love being measured back to us—"packed together, shaken down, and overflowing" (Luke 6:38).

Meditation: How are my Lenten disciplines helping me to be more aware of the love my Creator has put in me? How have I shared my gifts with others? Am I a cheerful giver? How have gifts returned to me?

Prayer: God of mercy and compassion, thank you for your many gifts. Free me to give as I have received.

True Authority

Readings: Isa 1:10, 16-20; Matt 23:1-12

Scripture:
"For they preach but they do not practice." (Matt 23:3)

Reflection: In today's Gospel Jesus shows respect for the office that the scribes and Pharisees hold, noting that they "have taken their seat on the chair of Moses." Their *instructions* are to be heeded, he says, but not their example.

There are different kinds of authority. There's the authority of office that comes with titles and built-in status. There's authoritarianism: authority for authority's sake, which quickly becomes self-serving. Then there's the authority that comes from within. This authority is seen in those whose words match their actions, who demonstrate trustworthiness, who lead by example.

Jesus is not against human authority or titles per se. If that were the case, it would be easy to fulfill his instruction in today's reading simply by not calling your dad "father" or your child's math instructor "teacher." But Jesus' point goes much deeper. He's asking us to see what true authority looks like and where it comes from. True authority acknowledges its source and its purpose. It comes from God and exists to serve God, not ourselves.

When Jesus sent his disciples on a mission, he "gave them authority" (Matt 10:1). He wants to empower us, too. We all have spheres of influence: among family members, in our workplace, with our friends. Do we want to be little dictators, serving only our own needs? Do we want to control others? Or do we see the rights and responsibilities of our positions, our status, and our titles as a way to serve God and our neighbor, and to bring more good into the world?

We can only do that when we have a sense of where our true status, our true importance, comes from: our identity as a child of God, a sister or brother of Christ, a vessel of the Holy Spirit. When our authority flows from that, we will lead and serve well.

Meditation: Where are my spheres of influence? How do I use the influence and status I've achieved? In what ways can I be a voice for the voiceless, an agent of positive change?

Prayer: Lord, help me serve you with whatever gifts and skills I have been given. In all my endeavors, may the glory be yours.

Deep Listening

Readings: Jer 18:18-20; Matt 20:17-28

Scripture:
"Can you drink the chalice that I am going to drink?" (Matt 20:22)

Reflection: Have you ever had the experience of talking to someone about something important to you, something serious, and then realizing the other person wasn't listening? Maybe when you stopped speaking, they just went on talking about themselves or another topic. If so, you probably felt let down. They didn't appreciate what you were saying, how vulnerable you were, or how significant this moment was for you.

Jesus confronts his disciples with the reality of where his mission is leading him. He tells them he will have to suffer. He's letting them into a mystery that's personal, pressing, and meaningful. What is he hoping for when he shares this? Support? Understanding? Is he inviting them into a deeper conversation?

The disciples' response offers much less than that. They seem oblivious to the reality and depth before them. They're too caught up in themselves. Two of them respond with total self-concern, trying to secure for themselves a special status in the kingdom to come. It's as if they didn't even hear what Jesus said.

And so Jesus must get back into teaching mode, telling the disciples what greatness in the kingdom looks like: not status, but service; not power, but innocence.

Are we so different from those first disciples? During Lent, we are confronted again with the depth of Christ's mystery. How do we respond? Do we go through life caught up only in ourselves, concerned only with our status, power, or possessions? Do we edit the word of God to hear only the rewards it promises, but not the demands it makes?

The apostles learned through Jesus' teaching and their own experiences. They did drink the same cup as Jesus, and they made themselves the servants of all. We will, too, as we allow ourselves to come before the Lord, listen to his words, and celebrate the depth of his mystery.

Meditation: In what ways do I "lord" my status or success over others? How do I feel when I'm more humble, more authentic? What can I do to practice a childlike openness to the gifts of life?

Prayer: Speak, Lord. Help me listen. Help me open my heart. Help me seek you in all things and places.

Life-Giving Roots

Readings: Jer 17:5-10; Luke 16:19-31

Scripture:
"[H]e was carried away by angels to the bosom of Abraham." (Luke 16:22)

Reflection: I like the distinction many people make between *individuality* and *individualism*. Individuality speaks to the uniqueness of a person. It is found in knowing and sharing one's gifts, pursuing one's goals, and actualizing one's potential. Individualism, though, is a turning in on oneself. It diminishes the self, eventually leading to a breakdown of the social connections and traditions that help people find meaning. People can find it difficult to commit to wider familial and communal structures. They begin to feel isolated and alienated.

The rich man in Jesus' parable can get all he wants within the gates of his own property. He enjoys his luxuries, but he does not seem to share them with anyone. For all we know, he dines alone every night. We do know that he could not connect with the person living right outside his door.

There are many forces that feed individualism. Developments in technology, for example, bring the world to our devices, while simultaneously making it easy to avoid the world. We must be intentional about fostering our communal identity. Our faith reminds us that we are rooted to what lies beyond us. We are connected to a tradition that reaches back thousands of years, to the bosom of Abraham. We are part of a faith community that stretches around the world and needs our presence and participation.

Jeremiah's image of the tree planted by the stream, bearing fruit even in dry times, is a beautiful picture of happiness. When forces of individualism entice us to retreat behind our gates and not even notice who is suffering at our doorstep, our roots can tap into a life-giving tradition that reminds us that we draw hope and strength from each other. Because we are deeply rooted, we will bear fruit for God and one another.

Meditation: How easy is it becoming for me to tune out the people I live with? My neighbors? Those in need? How do I participate in the life of my faith community?

Prayer: Forgive me, Lord, for failing to see how I can affect the lives of those around me for the better. Help me to care for others with humility and love.

Imagination and Dreams

Readings: Gen 37:3-4, 12-13a, 17b-28a; Matt 21:33-43, 45-46

Scripture:
They said to one another: "Here comes that master dreamer! Come on, let us kill him . . ." (Gen 37:19-20)

Reflection: You may recognize the words from Genesis above as the verse quoted on the memorial plaque at the motel where Martin Luther King, Jr., was assassinated: *Behold, here cometh the dreamer. . . .* It's dangerous to dream, and yet we can't help ourselves. Our dreams may be small or large, easily attainable or ambitious. The question is whether our dreams align with God's dream for us. Are they moving us toward the best in life? Are they rooted in love?

Our readings today depict dreamers and the rejection of their dreams. Jacob's son Joseph has dreams of becoming more than he is—a ruler, an agent of change. His brothers, driven by jealousy and hate, act to defeat his dreams. Jesus tells a story about a landowner who imagines a vineyard that will produce abundant fruit. But tenants who have been hired to work the vineyard instead wreak havoc and death because of their malice and greed.

Some may pity these dreamers because of the complacent or cruel forces that oppose them. Others will praise the divine spark in them. They have the audacity to imagine a different kind of world, a better life for themselves and others, a future of goodness and abundance. Our ability to dream—to imagine what does not yet exist and to move toward that vision—is a key to our humanity, our identity as creatures made in God's likeness. It is a source of our creativity and our daring.

Check up on your dreams. (They tend to evolve over time.) Are they aligned with God's dream for you? Are they, like those of Joseph and Jesus, rooted in the Father's love for you? Will they lead you to more health, holiness, peace, energy, and joy? Sometimes the opposition forces are not outside of us. Sometimes we are our own worst enemy, and our fears may defeat us. Are we stoking the love that overcomes fear?

Meditation: How am I exercising my power of imagination? What small dreams can I bring to life today? What large dreams are inspiring my work and my goals?

Prayer: God, help me be attentive to your voice. Inspire my dreams and put on my path those who can help me achieve them, for your glory.

Prodigal Love

Readings: Mic 7:14-15, 18-20; Luke 15:1-3, 11-32

Scripture:
"'[T]his son of mine was dead, and has come to life again; he was lost, and has been found.'" (Luke 15:24)

Reflection: St. Catherine of Siena is known for describing God as *pazzo d'amore*—"crazy in love" with us. Listening to Jesus' parables brings us to the same conclusion. The stories he tells right before today's parable of the Prodigal Son involve a shepherd risking everything to search for one lost sheep, and a woman turning her whole house upside down to find one little lost coin. When you're madly in love, you do things that others find hard to understand.

Some have suggested that today's parable—one of Jesus' most memorable—should be named the "Prodigal Father." The father is the one who's being wasteful and extravagant with his love: running out to meet his wayward son, embracing and kissing him, not letting him finish his penance speech, clothing him in fine robes, and throwing a huge party. The lost child has been found. What else matters?

Lent is an especially good time to celebrate the sacrament of reconciliation. God doesn't need it, but we do. When we feel lost, burdened, remorseful, afraid, or unable to forgive ourselves, our Father wants to give us a gift. He wants to embrace us. He wants to put a ring on our finger. He wants us to know that he has, as the prophet Micah wrote, "cast into the depths of the sea all our sins" (Mic 7:19).

There are other times when we're feeling strong, courageous, assured, and grateful for all God's gifts. That's when God wants us to come out to the road with him and be on the lookout for our lost brothers and sisters. God wants us to welcome them home and join the party, happy that they get to receive the same prodigal mercy, freedom, and joy that is always there for us.

Meditation: When have I been stingy or reluctant in offering mercy to others? What grudges do I need to let go of once and for all? Do I take time to appreciate God's "crazy love" for me?

Prayer: O Lord, you are the source of all mercy. Help me to live thankfully and joyfully because of the knowledge and experience of your love.

Thirst

Readings: Exod 17:3-7; Rom 5:1-2, 5-8; John 4:5-42 or 4:5-15, 19b-26, 39a, 40-42

Scripture:
"[W]hoever drinks the water I shall give will never thirst." (John 4:14)

Reflection: It all starts with a simple encounter, a simple request by Jesus: *Give me a drink.* It's a remarkable beginning to a conversation because it shouldn't have happened. Social and religious customs are being overstepped. But Jesus is thirsty. For water, yes, but his real thirst is for this Samaritan woman who has been judged by her neighbors, perhaps abandoned or used by men, probably ostracized from her own community. He seeks her faith. He wants her to know that she matters to God. He cares that she finds something that meets her thirst.

The woman starts out wary. She's learned to be tough and careful. What does this man really want? But as she listens to him, she sees his truthfulness, his compassion. He engages her respectfully and takes her seriously, including her in spiritual discourse. She recognizes that she is in the presence of a prophet. Walls fall. She allows him to see her as she is, to touch her on another level, the level of her thirst. She feels the spring of water he came to bring bubbling up within.

This conversation has become a breakthrough, and others need to know about it.

How many simple encounters fill our day? How many thirsts, hopes, needs do we encounter? Are we in touch with our own thirsts? How important can a true, authentic, loving conversation be?

Christ is seeking to converse with us. There's a spring of water ready to well up in us and overflow into worship. His own Spirit wants to come to us in our thirst, and flow from us to others who are thirsty.

Meditation: How have I experienced God meeting me in my thirsts? Where are the wells, the places of encounter in my life? Do I make time to go there and converse with my savior?

Prayer: O God, help me know what it means to worship you in Spirit and truth. Let any walls that keep me from letting you in fall. Let me be your instrument in a thirsty world.

Handling Rejection

Readings: 2 Kgs 5:1-15ab; Luke 4:24-30

Scripture:
"Amen, I say to you, no prophet is accepted in his own native place." (Luke 4:24)

Reflection: I once heard someone suggest that to keep a balanced perspective, you should have a dog that worships you and a cat that ignores you! A balanced perspective in life *is* important, but we don't usually have to seek out experiences that keep us humble. They tend to find us.

The wonder of the Incarnation is that God fully embraced our humanity. Jesus experienced all that we experience. That included experiences of appreciation from others who recognized his gifts. Crowds followed him, acclaimed him, accepted him as a prophet sent by God. He also experienced rejection and threats from religious and political leaders. Yet how must it have felt when people from his own hometown failed to value his wisdom and power? Familiarity can be an obstacle to recognizing what God is doing in our midst. But the fury of those in Nazareth who lashed out to the point of violence indicates an active refusal to hear Jesus' prophetic word.

How do we handle the experiences of dismissal or rejection that inevitably come our way? Do we wallow, or retreat, or lash out in kind? We can take a lesson from Jesus. First, he recognized who he was. He saw himself accurately, as part of the prophetic tradition of Israel, and accepted that his work would include reaching out to others who may oppose his message. Second, he didn't respond to others' rejection in kind, but "passed through the midst of them" (Luke 4:30). He did what he could, then went on to the next town, the next opportunity to share his gifts and fulfill his mission.

The next time we experience personal rejection, we don't have to get stuck in pain or negativity. We can remember who we are as children of God, believe in the prophetic word that Christ brought us, and move on with God's plan for our lives.

Meditation: How do I handle praise? How do I handle rejection? Do I ever miss the truths or blessings that God sends me in the familiar events and people in my life?

Prayer: Confirm me in my strengths, O Lord, and help me overcome my weaknesses, that I may move forward with humility and boldness.

Divine Generosity

Readings: Dan 3:25, 34-43; Matt 18:21-35

Scripture:
"'Should you not have had pity on your fellow servant, as I had pity on you?'" (Matt 18:33)

Reflection: One thing we may not catch in today's Gospel parable is how dire the servant's situation is when he approaches the king. Scholars point out that the amount the servant owes is a vast sum—more than he can possibly pay back in his whole lifetime. He may be in denial about that, but he knows it, and the king knows it, too. Therefore, when the king writes off the debt, he is giving the servant his very life back.

The thing is, the servant doesn't really appreciate the significance of what has happened. He doesn't comprehend the enormity of the gift that has been given to him. If he did, he wouldn't have approached his fellow servant in the way he did: stingily, vindictively. He demands payback for a pittance.

We could never pay God back for his divine generosity. We could never measure the amount of it. All of humanity was lost, and that includes us. We could never find our way out of that hole on our own. But in Christ, God poured out his life in mercy and forgiveness so that we could have another chance. We got our lives back. And we get our lives back every time we call on him.

If we realized that, we'd be free. If we really comprehended what has been given to us, we'd be liberated from our measured morality, our conditioned love, and the resentments we cling to. We wouldn't need them anymore. We'd be free, too, from the self-punishment we indulge in, from our unwillingness to forgive ourselves.

Today Jesus is inviting us to realize what we have been given, to remember what divine generosity has provided. Let's let it sink in. Then we will forgive as we have been forgiven. We will love as we are loved.

Meditation: When have I glimpsed the enormity of the divine gift in my life? When have I truly felt forgiven? When have I loved with God's generous love?

Prayer: O Lord, I believe in your mercy. Help my unbelief. Make me an instrument of your divine generosity and truth in the way I treat others.

Fulfilling the Law

Readings: Deut 4:1, 5-9; Matt 5:17-19

Scripture:
"Do not think that I have come to abolish the law or the prophets. I have come not to abolish but to fulfill." (Matt 5:17)

Reflection: In today's reading from Deuteronomy, Moses instructs the people on the law as they prepare to enter the Promised Land. He shares beautiful insights into the meaning of this communication of God to Israel and asks them, "For what great nation is there that has gods so close to it as the LORD, our God, is to us whenever we call upon him?" (Deut 4:7).

In the Gospel, Jesus states clearly that his teaching is no rejection of the law and prophets. Rather, it is his aim to bring their full meaning to light. Jesus builds upon and fulfills all that came before him. How do we interpret this fulfillment practically, say, when it comes to practicing religious traditions or making moral choices? How can living God's law help us find God's path in our daily life?

We are called neither to casualness nor rigidity toward the letter of the law. First, we can honor the traditions, customs, and laws that have been handed on to us, as they offer guidance and give us insight into doing good (even when we don't *feel* like doing good). Yet, we know that Jesus' prime concern was the *spirit* of the law. He was angered by those whose rigidity toward the law got in the way of others' salvation. He went beyond the letter to fulfill the heart of the law: judgment and mercy and fidelity (Matt 23:23). Jesus taught the spirit of the law which is love.

We follow a person, which is more challenging than following any law. Our morality is found in desiring the same Spirit that was in Jesus to be in us. And when it comes to deciding practical matters, knowing that our God is close to us opens the way to true discernment. Seeking the Lord in our hearts, staying close to Jesus in prayer, and being ready to follow his Spirit of love—this is our ultimate path and inspiration.

Meditation: What demands of Christian morality do I find most challenging? Where do I need more discipline in my life? Where do I need more Spirit-led freedom and spontaneity?

Prayer: Guide me, O Lord, that I may follow your commands and know your freedom. Help me to see in my Lenten disciplines a path to your love.

Falling

Readings: Jer 7:23-28; Luke 11:14-23

Scripture:
They walked in the hardness of their evil hearts / and turned their backs, not their faces, to me. (Jer 7:24)

Reflection: We can hear the discouragement in Jeremiah's words. The Lord keeps sending prophets who point out the way that leads to prosperity and life, but still the people fail to listen or correct their ways. They turn their faces from the right path.

Discouragement, struggle, and failure have their place in the spiritual life. I once heard the story of a visitor to an Eastern Orthodox monastery who was given a short tour by one of the brothers. After seeing some of the rooms and facilities, the visitor finally asked, "So, what do you monks actually *do* at the monastery?" The monk responded, "We fall and we get up, we fall and we get up . . . and we fall and we get up."

That may sound discouraging if we do not also know the encouragement, joy, and hope that are likewise part of the spiritual journey. This joy comes from including God in the process of growth that we call life. We may fall, but we get up! We advance in the Spirit. We grow as human beings by learning *how* to fall and rise. We unite our struggles to those of Jesus, turning our faces toward him.

A common Catholic devotion during Lent is the prayer service known as the Stations of the Cross. When we pray the Stations, we prayerfully accompany Jesus as he carries the cross to Golgotha. We imagine him falling once, twice, three times under its weight. Jesus identifies with us so we can identify with him. He shares in our humanity so we will find healing and growth as we share the journey with him. Then, like him, we not only get up, but we overcome.

Meditation: When have I felt discouraged in my walk with God? How did I handle it? What helped me get up from a fall? Have I seen how the pain of failure can lead to new insights and advancement?

Prayer: We adore you, O Christ, and we bless you. Because by your holy cross you have redeemed the world.

Two Commandments

Readings: Hos 14:2-10; Mark 12:28-34

Scripture:
"You shall love the Lord your God with all your heart. . . . You shall love your neighbor as yourself." (Mark 12:30-31; Deut 6:5; Lev 19:18)

Reflection: *What is the greatest commandment?* The scribe asks Jesus for only one commandment. But Jesus gives him two. He stands them side by side, interlocking the love of God and neighbor. He points out that we don't have one without the other.

Do we see this? What would the love of God be without the love of neighbor? An abstract idea? A nice feeling? An excuse to love in the abstract? Dorothy Day commented that it's easy to love "the world" or "humanity," but hard to love the flesh and blood sitting next to her on the bus. Loving people who have both strengths and weaknesses involves hard choices. It takes our time and demands our energy. But love must be found in the concrete, where we live, in flesh and blood.

We can ask the opposite as well: What would the love of neighbor be without the love of God? A label thrown around without substance or commitment? A product or transaction? Dependency or manipulation? Love involves perspective, freedom, and truth. True love comes with seeing ourselves as we are, through God's eyes, and seeing others as they are. It's the love of God that brings us to our center and clears our vision. Dependency and manipulation fall away. Then our love begins to participate in God's love for the other. We begin to see God in them.

With the love of God at our center, first in our souls, all else falls into its proper place, including our love for our neighbor.

Meditation: Have I ever used the word "love" for something that was less than love? How have I learned about the deeper meanings of love in my life? When has my love been tested? Can I see how God's love comes to me in my life experiences? How do I share the love that God has shared with me?

Prayer: Lord, I bring you my heart, my soul, my mind, my strength. Help me to bring your love to others and change the world with it.

In Need of Mercy

Readings: Hos 6:1-6; Luke 18:9-14

Scripture:

For it is love that I desire, not sacrifice,
and knowledge of God rather than burnt offerings.
(Hos 6:6)

Reflection: Jesus' parables are an artform. His stories invite us in so we can be shaken by God's truth, captured by God's love.

I once took a course with the famed Scripture scholar John Meier. I remember him saying that the people who first heard the parable of the Pharisee and the tax collector may have known they were being set up for something, but they would not have expected what was coming. In the parable, the Pharisee is doing everything right. He measures his obligations and even goes beyond what the law requires. The tax collector is practically a sinner by definition, collaborating with the hated Roman occupiers and probably a cheat. The Pharisee is just; the tax collector isn't.

The hearers, Meier imagined, knew a twist was coming. The nice rabbi, they thought, would say that the Pharisee would go home justified (right with God), and somehow God would work it out so the tax collector would, too. Somehow, he would "get by" because of God's mercy. They weren't prepared for the bigger surprise: The tax collector went home justified, but the Pharisee *didn't*. How could this be?

The Pharisee got it all right—on the outside. But he got it wrong on the inside. He missed out on what is most important, the thing that makes all the rest valuable and meaningful: love. The Pharisee used God to congratulate himself. He didn't even need God's mercy, or so he thought. The tax collector, on the other hand, brought nothing to God but himself. He knew who he was, and he knew he needed God. So he came to the temple honest, vulnerable, and transparent. And he was the one who left healed and changed. A transformation had begun.

Meditation: Do I try to get to God on my own power or by trying to be something I'm not? Or do I come to God by letting God come to me, as I am, letting his love work in me to heal and save?

Prayer: O God, be merciful to me, a sinner.

Seeing with the Heart

Readings: 1 Sam 16:1b, 6-7, 10-13a; Eph 5:8-14; John 9:1-41 or 9:1, 6-9, 13-17, 34-38

Scripture:
"Not as man sees does God see, because man sees the appearance but the Lord looks into the heart." (1 Sam 16:7)

Reflection: How often do our eyes deceive us? When it comes to evaluating situations or people, how often do we see only what we want to see?

David was left in the fields when the prophet Samuel came looking for a ruler. David was not mature enough, not strong enough, not ready. No one would look at him and see a king. But Samuel allowed himself to see with God's eyes, and he saw greatness.

When the Pharisees in John's Gospel looked at Jesus, they saw a troublesome figure, one who acted beyond the law, who extended God's favor to sinners and foreigners. They saw someone who challenged their influence and claimed authority that surely was not his. But the man born blind saw the one who touched his eyes, changed his perspective, and opened his mind. He perceived a revelation of God and bowed down to worship.

Some people see not just with their eyes. They see deeper, beyond appearances, to what is most real. They see with the heart. They see with God's eyes. And so they perceive others differently. They don't judge or dismiss or pass over them the way others might. They see themselves differently, too. They aren't tormented by others' gaze or ruled by fear. They see life differently. They savor the gift of life and share it with abandon.

The light for this kind of seeing is all around us. The man in today's Gospel story wasn't even looking for a healing. But the Light of the World sought him out and made him ready. We gather during Lent to hear Christ's word and share at his table. We gather so that his light will continue to break through to us—and through us to others.

Meditation: When have I felt lost in darkness or unable to find my way? When have I been blinded by appearances? When have I treated others carelessly? Where have I learned to look for God's light? How do I practice looking deeper, so this light can be shared with others?

Prayer: Open my eyes, Lord. Teach me your ways, lead me by your light, and help me to see others with my heart.

Believers

Readings: Isa 65:17-21; John 4:43-54

Scripture:
"You may go; your son will live." (John 4:50)

Reflection: The healing of the royal official's son was "the second sign Jesus did when he came to Galilee from Judea" (John 4:54). In John's Gospel, Jesus' healings and miracles are called "signs." Signs point to something. The invitation is to look beyond the supernatural occurrence to what it is saying to us. In other words, the point of miracles is not to ask "What happened?" but "What does it mean?"

The answer to that question is both mysterious and wonderful. Jesus restored health to a boy so he could live. He also restored the boy to his father and his family. Thus, the "whole household came to believe" (John 4:53). They *came to believe.* What does this mean? When we believe, our whole perspective on the gift of life shifts. The ups and downs, the joys and pain, the victories and defeats—all hold new meaning and promise. Life deepens and finds a goal.

We need not look to the extraordinary for life-altering signs. A young friend of mine recently told me of an experience he had in prayer before the Blessed Sacrament. He was seeking guidance about his vocation. The experience he related was not shocking, nor did it suspend the laws of nature.

But it was both mysterious and wonderful. It was the kind of experience that becomes a milestone, a signpost on the journey of life.

I'll bet you can search your personal history and see the signposts the Lord has sent to light your path and guide your journey. A common journaling exercise is to create a spiritual timeline. Draw a line with symbols representing your life: the peaks and valleys, experiences that have defined you, connections you've made, places where God taught you lessons and where you discovered meaning. Looking back on our lives and seeing the ways God has shined through to us is an experience we can all share as believers.

Meditation: How has God been present to me in the past? In extraordinary ways? In ordinary experiences? How has this affected my choices or supported my life as a believer?

Prayer: Lord, open my mind to understand how you come to me and offer me more life. Nurture my faith and strengthen my love.

Water from the Temple

Readings: Ezek 47:1-9, 12; John 5:1-16

Scripture:
[A]nd I saw water flowing out from beneath the threshold of the temple toward the east. (Ezek 47:1)

Reflection: Ezekiel's vison of water flowing from the sanctuary of the temple to irrigate the desert and provide food and medicine is a favorite image for retreat leaders. The temple of the soul is a dwelling of God whose life-giving nourishment flows from us to others and to a thirsty world.

Water flows through the Scriptures in both comforting and distressing manifestations. We are invited to lie beside restful waters (Ps 23), and then are tossed about in stormy seas (Mark 4:35-41). The waters of a great flood are destructive (Gen 7), while the waters of the Jordan announce the dawning of redemption (Matt 3:13-17).

I remember facilitating a college retreat where I incorporated a canoe trip down a placid creek that flowed through the retreat center's grounds. We enjoyed gently sailing along until low-hanging branches caused several of us to lose our balance and capsize! It was both harrowing and exhilarating, adding grist to our retreat reflections.

Sometimes the Lord holds us in a serene and fruitful embrace, attending to our need for solace and renewal. We peacefully float or glide along. At other times, as in the case of the man in today's Gospel reading who sits by the waters, lost in despondency and victimhood, God may essentially "splash" us with his grace. God urges us to wake up to the reality of our plight and the potential we are leaving unfulfilled. *Stop waiting for someone else to carry your weight*, Jesus pleads. *Get up and walk!*

This is the exhilarating water of the Spirit—the Spirit who calls us to acknowledge our power and its source, and encourages us to walk in faith and set sail in hope.

Meditation: Where am I in my relationship with God right now? Gently sailing along? Are waters getting rough? Or am I feeling the dryness of the desert? Do I need to return to the life-giving waters of the temple?

Prayer: Lord, send me your Spirit to stir up the waters within. Splash me with your grace. Grant me nourishment and healing. Enliven me and make me your instrument.

Mother and Father

Readings: Isa 49:8-15; John 5:17-30

Scripture:
But Zion said, "The LORD has forsaken me;
 my Lord has forgotten me."
Can a mother forget her infant,
 be without tenderness for the child of her womb?
 (Isa 49:14-15)

Reflection: Isaiah and Jesus offer us striking and poetic images today, invoking both a mother's and father's love. The words of Isaiah bring news of restoration and salvation to a people suffering in exile from their homeland. We can imagine how many of them may have stopped believing in God's help and care, saying, "The LORD has forsaken [us]." But Isaiah responds: "Can a mother forget her infant / . . . the child of her womb?" God's love for us echoes the most tender human love and beyond: "Even should she forget, / I will never forget you" (Isa 49:15).

We have trouble grasping a divine love that is beyond us, especially when we face discouragement and difficulty. But Jesus grasped it. Today and in the remaining days of Lent, we hear passages from John's Gospel that reflect Jesus' intimacy with the One he calls "Father." These passages speak strongly to the Christian understanding of God as Trinity.

The Holy Mystery at the center of the universe is both oneness and relationship. God is one, and God is love.

God, who is beyond us, sent his Word to embrace us in our humanity, to save us. In that embrace, God fills us with the Spirit, drawing us deeper into the divine life. God is this movement, this communion of love that we are invited into, and taken up into, through Christ.

If we only grasped how intimate God is to us, how all-encompassing God's love, then we wouldn't succumb to anguish or despair like those in exile. We would not be dragged down by the cynical or negative voices around us. Rather, we would "hear the voice of the Son of God" and live (John 5:25).

Meditation: When have I succumbed to feeling forsaken, forgotten, or ignored? Did I allow myself to hear the voice of the Lord at that time? What did God say?

Prayer: God of life, help me listen to your voice. When I am dejected or alone, bring me words of comfort and inclusion. When I'm joyful or content, confirm me with your words of everlasting life.

Journeys

Readings: 2 Sam 7:4-5a, 12-14a, 16; Rom 4:13, 16-18, 22; Matt 1:16, 18-21, 24a or Luke 2:41-51a

Scripture:
When Joseph awoke, he did as the angel of the Lord had commanded him and took his wife into his home. (Matt 1:24)

Reflection: We're all on a journey: from Abraham and Sarah, called into a new relationship with God; to Mary and Joseph, called to nurture a new creation; to each of us, choosing to walk forward with the Lord, trusting in God's promises and presence.

It's easy to overlook Joseph since, unlike Mary, he is not present from the beginning to the end of Jesus' journey. He is only at the beginning—but what a beginning! Like Mary, Joseph was chosen for his role and learned of it from an angel. Like Mary, he had to freely assent to his calling, even though he could not see clearly what the road ahead would look like. In the face of all the uncertainties and challenges, Joseph needed to discern the right way forward, perhaps even sacrificing his honor and reputation for the sake of his wife and child.

Like Mary, Joseph showed great strength, using all his wits and gifts in the role of protector and provider for his family. He was called to teach his son a trade as well as life lessons.

We can imagine what Jesus gleaned from Joseph's example, like the value of work and lessons of justice. When Jesus spoke of how a father wants to give good things to his children (Matt 7:9-11), was he recalling Joseph's character? Did he then relate those qualities to his experience of his heavenly Father?

On our own journeys we need traveling companions, including those who have gone before us. Our mothers and fathers in the faith have handed down an example to us. Like Joseph, may we too travel in courage and trust in the God who leads our way.

Meditation: How has my journey developed this Lent? Have I encountered challenges or opportunities to assent to God's will? Who have been good traveling companions for me?

Prayer: Almighty God, watch over and guide your church. May we, like St. Joseph, care well for those entrusted to us.

The Plot

Readings: Wis 2:1a, 12-22; John 7:1-2, 10, 25-30

Scripture:
"Let us condemn him to a shameful death;
for according to his own words, God will take care of him." (Wis 2:20)

Reflection: Detective stories, courtroom dramas, murder mysteries. . . . Audiences seem to love the psychological conflict, confrontation with uncertainty, and high stakes that these tales provide. They have in common the discovery of hidden clues, the unraveling of alibis, and a revealing of motivations. Evil plots are unveiled, and the guilty are exposed. Sometimes a person who was unjustly accused is vindicated. Case solved!

But there is not much mystery in the case of the "just one" in the book of Wisdom. We're immediately filled in on the motives of the unjust who seek to do evil. They beset this "son of God" because they think "he is obnoxious." His very presence annoys them. His awareness of his own identity confounds them. His way of life speaks judgement on them. And so they condemn him to a shameful death. Yet, as the book of Wisdom beautifully observes, they do not know "the hidden counsels of God" (Wis 2:22). Indeed, someone else is plotting in all of this: God.

Jesus is aware of those plotting against him. But in the face of that, he can say: "You know me and also know where I am from. Yet I did not come on my own, but the one who sent me, whom you do not know, is true" (John 7:28). It sounds like he's saying: *You think you know my origins, but there is more than the merely human at work here.* The "plotting" or plan of God will be seen in the end. All evil plotting will be unveiled, but so will the good that God intends.

The plot goes on. In whose story will we play our part? Are we plotting along with God's will for us—for our own good and for the healing of the world?

Meditation: How is my life different because I choose to follow Christ? Have I had to sacrifice anything for this choice? How have I grown as a person because of it? How are the people around me enriched by it?

Prayer: Good and loving God, I want to play my part in your eternal story. I want to live the adventure of faith with you as my guide and deliverer.

Division

Readings: Jer 11:18-20; John 7:40-53

Scripture:
Yet I, like a trusting lamb led to slaughter, had not realized that they were hatching plots against me: "Let us destroy the tree in its vigor; let us cut him off from the land of the living." (Jer 11:19)

Reflection: It's easy to tell people what they want to hear. It's harder to confront them when they've done something wrong. But that's just what prophets do. Not only do they offer the consoling word of God amid people's pain and distress; they also deliver God's rebuke in the face of evil intentions and violations of God's precepts. Needless to say, prophets get on the nerves of those they challenge.

According to tradition, the prophets Jeremiah, Isaiah, Ezekiel, Micah, and Amos all suffered martyrdom. They did not tell the powerful what they wanted to hear. But many people did recognize the divine call in their words and gestures, and they collected and preserved the prophets' words for future generations. These prophetic books continue to be a source of divine encounter, comfort, and judgement for those of us who read them today. God continues to speak through them.

Jesus, coming out of this prophetic tradition of Israel, experienced what many of the prophets before him did. In today's passage from John's Gospel, we see the division among religious leaders caused by Jesus' teaching and actions. Some, like Nicodemus, are open to hearing more from Jesus and to accepting the divine origins of his message. Others are nitpicking about his earthly origins in order to dismiss and condemn him.

Jesus once said: "I have come to set the earth on fire. . . . Do you think that I have come to establish peace on the earth? No, I tell you, but rather division" (Luke 12:49, 51). The prophetic word always invites a choice. What values will guide our path? What vision of life will we embrace? What possibilities will we leave behind? Whose kingdom will we serve?

Meditation: What life-altering decisions have I made to align myself with the values of God's kingdom? Have I made any significant choices for my life this Lent?

Prayer: Lord, strengthen my resolve and give me courage to follow you in all circumstances. May your light guide me and your arm hold me close.

No Boundaries

Readings: Ezek 37:12-14; Rom 8:8-11; John 11:1-45 or 11:3-7, 17, 20-27, 33b-45

Scripture:
So Jesus said to them, "Untie him and let him go."
(John 11:44)

Reflection: Several Sunday Gospel passages this Lent have searched for ways to describe the indescribable: the effect of Christ in our lives. When words fail us, we turn to images, symbols, poetry, and signs. For the Samaritan woman, there was the sign of water, an unfailing font quenching thirst from within. For the man born blind, there was light, a new brilliance that brings awareness, clarity, and depth.

Now, for Lazarus, life itself was the sign. Lazarus's life had come to an end. His remains were locked behind stone, bound by burial cloth. Can we see in Lazarus's lifelessness an image of life without meaning and hope, without worth and inner freedom? Do we detect a despair that cannot be bridged, a boundary that cannot be crossed? But God's saving will knows no boundaries.

What keeps us bound? What needs to be untied? For some of us it is a painful experience from the past or the inability to move beyond grief. For others it is an aversion to risk and reluctance to grow. For still others it is the tyranny of other people's expectations or the weight of unforgiveness. The shackles are many. The gloom of our status quo can seem undefeatable.

And yet, in the midst of pain, worry, fear, pride, and every other form of lifelessness that keeps us trapped or immobilized, we detect a spark of life that calls us beyond what binds us. We sense a promise that offers us fullness of life. We hear a voice that stands out against every other: "Untie him. Untie her. Let them go."

Meditation: When have I felt fully alive? When have I felt only half-alive? When have I felt dead? Where do I go, or what do I do, to welcome Christ's life into mine, to heal and revive me?

Prayer: From the depths, I cry to you, O Lord. Break the chains that keep me from living the life you are calling me to live. Let your light break through any gloom. Let me feel the stirrings of hope within me.

Spirit of Mercy

Readings: Dan 13:1-9, 15-17, 19-30, 33-62 or 13:41c-62; John 8:1-11

Scripture:
So he was left alone with the woman before him. (John 8:9)

Reflection: Literal stoning of those who break the law, religious or not, still happens in some parts of the world. And it happens everywhere figuratively. It is not much of a leap to imagine ourselves in the story of Jesus with the woman caught in the act of adultery.

Maybe we know what it's like to be among those who are pointing their fingers—the ones who accuse, condemn, or think of themselves as superior. We can be honest about this, admitting it is not in the spirit of Jesus. It's interesting that many of the greatest saints speak of themselves as the greatest sinners. They are not being disingenuous; they see their great need for God's mercy. And they see their need as part of humanity's great need. They see that, in the end, all is grace. One of Mother Teresa's most familiar quotes is: "If you judge others, you have no time to love them." Love, not judgment, is in the spirt of Jesus.

But perhaps we also know what it is like to have the fingers pointing at us. Perhaps we have been the accused, the excluded, the judged. When Jesus and the woman are finally alone, we see again what the spirit of Jesus is like. It is love, understanding, mercy. Sensing this, she can allow Jesus to see her. She can hear his words to her.

During Lent, we are reminded of our need for mercy and of the Lord's desire to come to us and teach us that we have nothing to fear. Can we allow ourselves to be seen by the One who knows us as we are and loves us as we are?

What healing and growth will spring from that! It will change everything.

Meditation: Where in my life am I tempted to judge harshly and then throw stones? Do I challenge myself to see others with Christ's eyes? In what ways do I allow myself to come into the Lord's gaze, to be known and loved?

Prayer: God of mercy, keep me aware of your constant care for me. Share with me deeper insights into myself and our relationship. Grant me patience and concern for others who need your mercy.

A Sign of Healing

Readings: Num 21:4-9; John 8:21-30

Scripture:
Moses accordingly made a bronze serpent . . . and whenever anyone who had been bitten by a serpent looked at [it], he lived. (Num 21:9)

Reflection: When Moses lifts up the bronze serpent and people are healed, it is not magic. Instead, Moses is using a sign or symbol to communicate a truth that will open a path to healing. But what is the truth the sign is pointing to? Why ask the people to look at a serpent, when serpents were the original cause of their misery?

We often avoid looking at the very thing that is causing us pain. It's uncomfortable to accept and examine the dark places within us. Instead, we tend to repress and deny. We pretend there is no darkness and that we have no problems, no flaws. We project our strength and deny our weakness.

Our relationship with God is not immune to this. We want to be perfect. We defend ourselves instead of honestly appraising our lives before God. But if we do this, we don't face up to our real situation with honesty and vulnerability. If we stay in that place, we won't come to the awareness that the people of Israel came to in the desert, when Moses led them to repent and return to their relationship of trust in God.

"When you lift up the Son of Man, then you will realize that I AM" (John 8:28). When John's Gospel speaks of Jesus being "lifted up," it is referring to the cross. No one wants to look at the terrible reality of the cross, its pain and misery. The cross is the result of a sinful world doing its worst to the sinless one. But Jesus brought God's love and mercy and power there.

The cross is the sign of ultimate healing. Let's look upon it and let God heal us.

Meditation: What do I see when I look at a cross or crucifix? Is it a sign of something that is beyond my own power to restore and save? In what ways have I followed Christ to find healing in body, mind, or spirit?

Prayer: Lord, I come before you as I am, strengths and weaknesses together. Let me embrace what is most real so I can be a channel of your truth and healing to others.

The Jewel

Readings: Isa 7:10-14; 8:10; Heb 10:4-10; Luke 1:26-38

Scripture:
"Behold, I am the handmaid of the Lord. May it be done to me according to your word." (Luke 1:38)

Reflection: Celebrating the feast of the Annunciation during Lent may bring a feeling of disconnection. After all, our thoughts are rightly turning to Holy Week. Our concern is to accompany the adult Christ through his final days. Our minds are on Jerusalem, not Nazareth.

And yet it is fitting that at this turning point we return to the beginning of the whole story. Because it is all one mystery—Jesus' birth, ministry, passion, death, resurrection, ascension, and the sending of the Spirit—encompassing the one truth of Christ's saving work for us. It is one jewel with many facets that we keep turning to catch the light in different ways. We do so to appreciate its magnitude, its beauty, and its power to speak to our own multi-faceted lives. We grow and learn from each of those facets as they touch our experiences, our needs, and our readiness to comprehend.

Our mother and sister Mary was there at the beginning, the middle, and the end of the story. From Bethlehem and Nazareth, to Cana, to the foot of the cross and the Upper Room, she walked the path of discipleship. She knew the joys of new beginnings, the sorrow and pain of rejection and grief, and the glories of passing over to new life. But it all began with simple trust and receptivity, a joyful yet risky seizing of the graced moment, an honest "May it be . . ."

As we pass through this one mystery, with its joyful steps and painful stretching, may we do so as Mary did, with faithful trust, all leading to glory.

Meditation: What facets of the mystery of Christ speak to me at this time in my life? How have my experiences of joy or sorrow brought me closer to God? How have I brought the message of salvation to others?

Prayer: Hail Mary, full of grace, the Lord is with thee. Blessed art thou among women and blessed is the fruit of thy womb, Jesus. Holy Mary, Mother of God, pray for us sinners, now and at the hour of our death. Amen.

Called by Name

Readings: Gen 17:3-9; John 8:51-59

Scripture:
Jesus said to them, "Amen, amen, I say to you, before Abraham came to be, I AM." (John 8:58)

Reflection: Words are important. They bring about change. They can build up or tear down. One word that is particularly powerful for each of us is our name. Hearing our name can be moving and meaningful. When we come to an awareness of being known and called by God, we might express it as feeling called by name.

There are moments in Scripture when people are so touched by God's power that they are given a new name. The divine activity in their life brings a new sense of identity and mission. In the book of Genesis, Abram becomes "Abraham" and Sarai becomes "Sarah" when God establishes a covenant with them and their descendants.

Because that covenant was made with human beings, it has had its ups and downs. Sometimes God's people were weak and stumbled in their commitments. But God remained faithful. Sometimes they grew weary of the covenant's demands. Sometimes they turned away and violated the covenant. Yet God continued to remain faithful. God was so faithful that, in the fullness of time, God sealed the covenant in flesh and blood. God came to us in person to save us.

In John's Gospel, Jesus gives himself a name: "I AM." He is intentionally recalling the divine name given to Moses (Exod 3:14). God comes to us in Jesus, embraces us in our humanity, and welcomes us into a new covenant, a new relationship of intimacy with the divine. And even though we may still stumble or fall away, God remains faithful, continually coming to our aid, moving us forward to new life.

Meditation: When have I felt honored or moved by the calling of my name? When has hearing my name brought a sense of peace or purpose? What moments bring me into a deeper awareness that I am known and loved by the God of the universe?

Prayer: Glory be to the Father, and to the Son, and to the Holy Spirit, as it was in the beginning, is now, and will be forever.

Stones

Readings: Jer 20:10-13; John 10:31-42

Scripture:
"I have shown you many good works from my Father. For which of these are you trying to stone me?" (John 10:32)

Reflection: Today's Gospel once again shows us that Jesus' ministry is rooted in the prophetic tradition of Israel. Prophets freely speak the words and messages God gives them. These words are not always what people *want* to hear, but they are what they *need* to hear. And so prophets are often opposed. Like Jeremiah in the Old Testament, Jesus experiences rejection. The people are unsettled by a message that calls them out of familiar ways of thinking about God and out of established patterns that bring stability and comfort.

But before we criticize those who picked up stones against Jesus, we had better examine ourselves. At whom would we be ready to "cast stones" today? Whose words cut to our hearts and call us out of our comfort zones and complacency? Whose lives and moral examples call us to be more faithful to Gospel values? Do we find ourselves resisting those calls and examples? How can we be more open to the invitation to be more Christ-like in dealing with the world around us? Or, even more challenging, how are we following in the prophetic footsteps of Jesus?

Jesus gives us a hint into where the prophet's resilience is fostered and where his inspiration is fed. After the crowd's effort to stone Jesus fails, we're told that he "went back across the Jordan to the place where John first baptized, and there he remained" (John 10:40). Jesus goes back to the beginning. He returns to the place where he initiated his ministry in the waters of new birth, where the Spirit descended upon him and affirmed his mission. Here is where he heard the Father declare: "You are my beloved" (Mark 1:11).

As disciples, there are times when we too need to return to our beginnings, to remember our call and steady our commitment. The sacred times, places, persons, and memories God has provided for us will come to our aid. The Spirit will envelop us. And no stone will harm us.

Meditation: Who has had a prophetic influence in my life? What times or places has God used to break through to me and call me to discipleship?

Prayer: Come, Holy Spirit.

One Shepherd

Readings: Ezek 37:21-28; John 11:45-56

Scripture:
[T]here shall be one shepherd for them all. . . . I will make with them a covenant of peace; it shall be an everlasting covenant with them. (Ezek 37:24, 26)

Reflection: The prophet Ezekiel lived through a tragic time in the history of God's chosen people. Their failure to listen to God's word resulted in pain and ruin. Exiled in Babylon, they experienced discouragement and suffering. Yet Ezekiel's book ends with a vision of hope in what God will accomplish through it all. The scattered peoples will be gathered. A new Jerusalem will rise from the ruins. And one shepherd will guide them.

Our personal stories likely include times of discouragement as well. We too have failed to listen. We've fallen on our chosen path. We may have even sunk into ruin at times, wondering if there is any future for us. This discouragement would be the end of the story if we did not also know the encouragement, the hope, and the joy that come from including God in our story. In our process of spiritual growth, we advance in the Spirit and grow as human beings by learning from the one Shepherd who has arrived and is at the gates of Jerusalem.

As Lent begins to wind down and we prepare to enter Holy Week, the rhythms of our communal prayer begin to shift. We've traveled together through a kind of desert, hoping to strip away attachments that hinder our growth. We've remembered God's promises of healing and received God's blessings that come to us every day. Now we prepare to walk again with Jesus through his final days, to experience the turning point of human history and to renew our covenant with our saving God.

Meditation: What has Lent meant for me this year? What has God taught me? Have I faced obstacles or challenges? Have I experienced the Lord's consolation? How can I approach Holy Week in an attentive and prayerful way?

Prayer: Prepare my heart, Lord Jesus, to accompany you through the mystery of your final days. May your Spirit shepherd me through the darkness of my suffering into the light of your presence. May I know your covenant of peace.

Armed Only with the Spirit

Readings: Matt 21:1-11; Isa 50:4-7; Phil 2:6-11; Matt 26:14–27:66 or 27:11-54

Scripture:
And when he entered Jerusalem the whole city was shaken and asked, "Who is this?" (Matt 21:10)

Reflection: Flashback: A middle eastern city, two millennia ago, filled with contradictions and strong emotions. Amid a hated military occupation, opposing political camps exist in a tense standoff. Religious parties debate different understandings of spiritual values. Most people are probably going about their lives, trying to support themselves and their families, praying for peace, hoping for the best.

Jesus enters the city, riding on a donkey, armed only with the Spirit. Some are ready to welcome him and hear his words as he taps into their emotions and hopes. They long for a better life and world; they desire an answer to their deepest questions. At the same time, as Jesus must know, there are those who are hostile to him. They may be afraid of his large crowds or offended by his closeness with God and the freedom it gives him. *If he's smart,* those people might have said, *he'll stay away, especially this week when the city is so crowded and tense.* But he didn't stay away. He came for them—all of them.

Fast forward: Today. We've come so far, learned so much, grown in so many ways. Yet still the world is full of contradictions and strong emotions. Some are happy as they plan their futures or find new opportunities. Some are in pain as they face personal difficulties and uncertainty. Some despair amid societal polarization and warring factions. Most are just trying to go about their daily lives, hoping for a better future, seeking peace and purpose.

Jesus comes again today, armed only with the Spirit. As we tell his story this week, let's be among those who welcome him.

Meditation: How will I make this week special? When can I take time to pray and reflect on the Passion reading? Can I enter the story in a new way, maybe by identifying with a particular character? How do I see myself walking with Christ in my daily life?

Prayer: Lord God, strengthen me as I follow you through difficult times in my life. Help me to more deeply experience the new life you came to bring.

The Fragrance of Love

Readings: Isa 42:1-7; John 12:1-11

Scripture:
Mary took a liter of costly perfumed oil made from genuine aromatic nard and anointed the feet of Jesus and dried them with her hair; the house was filled with the fragrance of the oil. (John 12:3)

Reflection: In 2019, people around the globe watched heartbreaking scenes of fire sweeping through Notre Dame Cathedral in Paris. Commentators reminded us of the storied history of the twelfth-century edifice and remarked on the sublime beauty of its medieval architecture and striking windows. I was surprised to learn that at some point in the nineteenth century, the cathedral was in such disrepair that some suggested its demolition. It was a literary artist, Victor Hugo, who encouraged Parisians to safeguard the world treasure in their midst.

Why do works of art like Notre Dame matter? They're impractical after all. People often question why the money wasn't put to work for practical concerns or to help those in real need. But there are different human needs, and those who are poor or marginalized are not one-dimensional. They have different needs, too, and are often excluded from beautiful spaces inhabited by elites, or places where one needs to buy a ticket or "be somebody" to enter. The doors of the church need to be opened to welcome everyone into beauty.

In today's Gospel, Mary of Bethany pours out expensive perfumed oil to express her love and devotion to Jesus. Fragrance fills the house. She wastes her resources and herself, and she's attacked for the extravagance. But Jesus defends her. He defends this human need, and the healing that comes from love, devotion, and beauty.

Holy Week brings a lot of extravagant activity to churches. Time, planning, resources—all are "wasted." We're invested in making beautiful things for God, an act of love for the One who loves us, and who poured out his life to set us free. We want that fragrance to fill the house.

Meditation: What works of art are special to me? How have they touched my spirit or strengthened me to act in new ways? How am I using my own creative gifts to affect the world around me?

Prayer: Lord Jesus, Anointed One of God, send your creative Spirit to inspire me. Help me to see good that doesn't yet exist and to move toward it. May I offer something beautiful to you.

The Way Out

Readings: Isa 49:1-6; John 13:21-33, 36-38

Scripture:
Reclining at table with his disciples, Jesus was deeply troubled and testified, "Amen, amen, I say to you, one of you will betray me." (John 13:21)

Reflection: The disciples are surprised by Jesus' announcement of a betrayer. Apparently, they didn't have a clue what was coming based on the words or actions of Judas, though they had lived and traveled with him for some time.

What we nurture in our hearts, though, will eventually make its way into our actions. We might wonder what festered in the heart of Judas that ultimately led to his downfall. Was it confusion over his expectations of the Messiah or a desire to bring about a confrontation with the authorities? Or was it a change in loyalties, a yearning to be accepted by those same authorities who opposed Jesus? Or was it some deep-seated pain or suffering that turned into an ugly distortion, a rejection of Judas's best self?

Judas's true intentions remain a mystery. What is not a mystery is that Jesus washed the feet of his betrayer at the Last Supper. He came to Judas and performed the same shocking act of service that he did for the others he loved. Something in Judas may have changed, but Jesus' love didn't. How tragic that Judas didn't come to realize this!

C. S. Lewis, in his book *The Problem of Pain*, famously wrote that "the doors of hell are locked on the *inside*" (HarperCollins, 1996, p. 130). How often in our own pain or suffering do we seek to lock the door and keep others out? How often have we felt that we're too far gone, that there's no use trying again, or that there's no way we can come back after the mess we've made? How have we felt lost or trapped?

The story of Jesus' final days reminds us that, despite our locked doors, he will always come to our side. He'll get on his knees to cleanse, heal, and refresh us. He opens the doors, delivering a way out of hell.

Meditation: When have I nurtured what I knew was a wrong impulse in me? When have I felt like my failures were too much to bear? How did I return to the God of light and hope?

Prayer: O Lord, our Lenten journey has brought me here again, to an awareness of my needs and your compassion. Give me the humility and courage to always call upon you for help.

Morning after Morning

Readings: Isa 50:4-9a; Matt 26:14-25

Scripture:
Morning after morning
he opens my ear that I may hear;
And I have not rebelled,
have not turned back. (Isa 50:4-5)

Reflection: A person's character shines in the great moments of life: the tests of will, the moments of truth, the milestone events that are remembered. These events crown one's lifespan. But character is made in the small, hidden, mundane moments and challenges that come "[m]orning after morning." The crown is forged in the daily grind, the unsung choices, the decisions to follow one's path and to honor one's values when no one else is noticing. It's shaped when we get up to get the kids to school, work on projects, shop for dinner, or make ourselves available when a friend is in need.

Jesus could have played it safe that week in Jerusalem. He could have laid low, left town, hidden from the crowds. He could have changed his tone, stopped teaching and acting the way he did. He could have flattered the authorities and told them what they wanted to hear. He could have saved his life. Instead, he kept doing what he always did. He stayed true to himself, faithful to his Father, committed to those he came to save.

Jesus was the Servant the prophet Isaiah speaks of in today's first reading. Daily he opened his ear to God's word. He spoke words to rouse the weary and was unflinching in the face of opposition. When others rose against him with insults and beating, he did not turn back but trusted in God's help. He was strong and loving to the end. And he did it all for those who denied him, betrayed him, and fled from him.

If we ever feel our trials are too small, our challenges too mundane, or our daily tasks insignificant, we can remember that character is made there. We can know that God is preparing us for great moments and shaping us to be faithful servants like his Son.

Meditation: How has this Lent shaped me? What were some of the small moments that affected me or allowed me to change?

Prayer: O God, help me to see the small events in my life as opportunities to learn and grow in love for you. Prepare me to take on the tests that life will bring. Help me to always remain faithful to you.

Endings and Beginnings

Readings: Exod 12:1-8, 11-14; 1 Cor 11:23-26; John 13:1-15

Scripture:
He loved his own in the world and he loved them to the end. (John 13:1)

Reflection: Endings are difficult. Maybe you've had the experience of leaving home, changing jobs, saying goodbye to a loved one. Moments like these, even if small, are meaningful, perhaps bittersweet. They call for both words and gestures, signs and symbols.

Think of Jesus and the disciples at their last meal. They had spent so much time together. They traveled together, shared many meals, listened to many stories. Jesus shared his teaching about the kingdom of God with them. He shared silence with them. He included them in his ministry of healing and sent them off on special missions. He showed them what it's like to confront hypocrisy and break out of old patterns of thought.

And now Jesus knows it is ending. How will he share the meaning of it all in a way they can remember, in a way that resonates with their deepest hopes? First, he enacts a stunning act of service. The foot washing is not merely a humble deed, but a sign that points to the meaning of his final hour: a reversal of roles, a divine emptying for the sake of our salvation, as well as an example to follow. Then he gives them the perpetual memorial that has been "handed on" to us (1 Cor 11:23). He gives his whole self, the gift we receive at his table.

In all this, we disciples are not just observers. To accept Jesus in his saving role is to become a participant, a sharer in his risen life. He becomes the pattern we follow, the power that frees us to serve. Now we can bring hope to our struggling world. Now we can teach and heal and announce our salvation in Christ. Now, each day, we can begin.

Meditation: How has my understanding or appreciation of the gift of the Eucharist grown over the years? How can I be more sensitive to the needs of God's people around me so I can serve them? To the needs of the world so I can bring hope?

Prayer: Lord, you have commanded us to do for each other as you have done for us. Give me a humble reliance on your presence and strength in my life so I may always follow your example of service and compassion.

The Mystery of the Cross

Readings: Isa 52:13–53:12; Heb 4:14-16; 5:7-9; John 18:1–19:42

Scripture:
We had all gone astray like sheep,
each following his own way;
but the LORD laid upon him
the guilt of us all. (Isa 53:6)

Reflection: There's a retreat center I like to visit along the Connecticut coast. It has a unique cross that sits atop its chapel. The place where the horizontal and vertical arms come together is not solid, but an open space you can see through. I think of it as an opening for me and every person to enter. I see a birth canal into the mystery of the cross.

As a mystery, the cross is not something we simply "figure out" all at once. There's not just one thing we can learn about it. It can't be easily defined. We need to live with it. The cross gets planted in our lives and grows in significance as we bring our experiences to it. It's a mystery we continue to participate in.

The cross brings us to the threshold of divine wisdom and power. The story it tells is not morbid. It is not the result of a vengeful deity who needs to be appeased in some way. Rather, the cross is the story of a God who so loved the world that he sent his Son. It's about God who so loved the world that he didn't stay distant from it but entered into it—all of it, good and bad—for the sake of our healing.

This is how sin or death or anything that can oppress human beings can be overcome: through the love of God that we see poured out on the cross. We receive that love as a gift and can now bring it into any situation, no matter how broken. Think of anything you've gone through or are going through right now—questions, doubts, pain, uncertainty, hope. Do you think we have a God who understands? Who walks with us? Who will never abandon us? Look to the cross.

Meditation: How has the cross been planted in my life? What am I bringing to the cross this year in my prayer, meditation, and worship? How can I help others in my life carry their crosses?

Prayer: Into your hands, O Lord, I commend my spirit. Protect me by your power. Teach me your wisdom. Help me to persevere. And, with Christ, welcome me into your glory.

Strong and Gentle

Readings: Gen 1:1–2:2 or 1:1, 26-31a; Gen 22:1-18 or 22:1-2, 9a, 10-13, 15-18; Exod 14:15–15:1; Isa 54:5-14; 55:1-11; Bar 3:9-15, 32–4:4; Ezek 36:16-17a, 18-28; Rom 6:3-11; Matt 28:1-10

Scripture:
She [wisdom] is the book of the precepts of God,
  the law that endures forever;
all who cling to her will live. . . .
Turn, O Jacob, and receive her:
  walk by her light toward splendor. (Bar 4:1-2)

Reflection: This is a day of contrasts. Tonight, at the Easter Vigil, the church's prayer starts in darkness. A single flame rises from the Paschal candle. We follow it as it moves through the darkness, piercing the night. As big as the darkness feels, it cannot overcome that light. That little flame, so small yet so powerful, so strong yet so gentle, draws us to its light, and draws us together. The light has a mission: to share itself, to spread its reach, to touch minds and hearts, to create more light.

Today I think of Mary, the mother of Jesus, after the crucifixion. What did she do this day when the tomb was closed? How did she pray? Did she ponder the psalms as her son did from the cross, saying "My God, my God, why have you abandoned me?" (Ps 22:2) and "Into your hands I commend my spirit" (Ps 31:6)? And I think of the other women, Mary Magdalene and the other Mary (Matt 28:1), who waited for the Sabbath to be over so they could go to the tomb. They waited and they prepared, these friends of God, guided by holy Wisdom (Wis 7:27).

The church prays alongside these women on this night, as we recount stories of blessing and sacrifice, of rescue and calling. And with them we feel the earth shake. The gentle light that has moved on the waters from the beginning of time now breaks through like lightning, in heavenly brightness! The Spirit breathes on the baptismal font. "Alleluias" are sung. The risen life that overcame sin and death touches us and brings us to life in a new way. We begin to see ourselves anew: *forgiven, blessed, loved.*

Light shines. Darkness flees. And the mission begins—to spread the strong and gentle light of Christ to others.

Meditation: How do I pray when I'm feeling overwhelmed or when I'm waiting for God to speak to me? How do I ask God to strengthen my hope and sustain my life with divine light?

Prayer: Brighten my days, O Lord. Help me to be gentle with the wounded and strong with those who need your guidance. Breathe in me, that I may rejoice in your Spirit all my days.

The Heart of It All

Readings: Acts 10:34a, 37-43; Col 3:1-4 or 1 Cor 5:6b-8; John 20:1-9 or Matt 28:1-10

Scripture:
They both ran, but the other disciple ran faster than Peter and arrived at the tomb first. (John 20:4)

Reflection: Is what we celebrate today a matter of the head or the heart? In the face of the bafflement and trauma of seeing their teacher and friend crucified, the disciples experienced something that changed them forever. It was something that brought them from grief to joy, from despair to faith. And the only way they could talk about it was to preach the good news: God had raised Jesus, and they had encountered him alive!

This was not merely a "head thing," nor was it ultimately about convincing. It was and is ultimately about the heart. By that I don't mean mere emotion. When the Bible speaks about the heart, it means the center of the person—mind, intellect, emotion, will—the integration of the whole self. The heart is the center of who we are.

Peter and the "other disciple" ran to the tomb. Elsewhere in John's Gospel, this "other disciple" is called the "Beloved Disciple." Although we traditionally consider John to be the Beloved Disciple, John's Gospel never identifies him. Some have suggested that John doesn't name this disciple because he wants each of us to identify with him. He wants each of us to see ourselves as the beloved. In any case, this "other disciple" gets to the tomb first. Is it because he's younger? Or is it because he's beloved? Love gets there first. Love runs.

Jesus went to his death believing in the Father's love. He brought God's love and mercy to the cross, into sin and death, to overcome it. God raised Jesus from the dead and will raise us up with him. The apostles went to their deaths witnessing to this message. Why? Not for a proposition or an argument but for a Person, for the Love they encountered that freed them.

That Love is alive for us right now, and we celebrate that today with all our heart.

Meditation: How will I celebrate on this day of days? How will I consciously extend my celebration into the whole Easter season and beyond?

Prayer: Risen Lord, open my heart to your message and your reality. May it free me to live the new life you came to bring.